W9-CII-021

ZEN JUDAISM

Teaching Tales by a Kabbalistic Rabbi

ZEN JUDAISM

Teaching Tales by a Kabbalistic Rabbi

JOSEPH H. GELBERMAN, Ph.D.
WITH LESLEY SUSSMAN

ILLUSTRATIONS BY CATHERINE ROSE CROWTHER

THE CROSSING PRESS
FREEDOM, CALIFORNIA

Cover design by Petra Serafim

Interior design by Abi Cotler
Printed in the U.S.A.

For information on bulk purchases or group discounts for this and other Crossing Press titles, please contact our Special Sales Director at 800/777-1048 ext. 203.
Visit our Web site: www.crossingpress.com

Library of Congress Cataloging-in-Publication Data

Gelberman, Joseph H.
Zen Judaism : teaching tales by a kabbalistic rabbi / by Joseph Gelberman / with Lesley Sussman.
p. cm.
ISBN 1-58091-095-5 (pbk.)
1. Gelberman, Joseph H.--Anecdotes. 2. Rabbis--United States--Anecdotes. 3. Hasidim--United States--Anecdotes. I. Title.
BM755.G4225 A25 2001
296.1'9--dc21

2001042387
CIP

0 9 8 7 6 5 4 3 2 1

Dedicated to almighty God and Rebbe Nachman of Breslov, whose whole message was one of joy.

I want to thank my dear friends, Dr. Dorothy Kobak, Ph.D., Pamela Bloom, and David Obregon, who helped me collect many of these stories over the years. I also want to thank Les Sussman who worked with me on my last book, *Physician of the Soul.* He has been a source of encouragement to me. And let me not forget my beautiful wife, Jan, as well as my wonderful agent and dear friend, Claire Gerus.

Know that a person
walks through life
on a very narrow bridge.
The most important thing
is not to be afraid.

—Rebbe Nachman of Breslov

Introduction

It is the story more than any other source of Jewish literature that best communicates the religious and ethical messages of Judaism. Even the most unlearned person can understand a story—that is why it was the teaching tool of the Baal Shem Tov, the founder of the Hasidic movement. I grew up in the Hasidic tradition where story telling was always part of the Sabbath services when the rabbi told a story by way of teaching his congregation. The stories came either from his own life, from the Talmud, or from another Judaic religious text. Most of the great rabbis over the centuries have taught their people through stories. Jesus taught his flock this way, as did Krishna, Buddha, and Mohammed. It's a more interesting way to illuminate the path.

ONE TIME, MAYBE A COUPLE OF YEARS ago, A well known professor in the United States decided to travel to India to study with a guru. Now this is strange since the professor, like many of us, believed he knew so much he really didn't need advice from anybody. Well, after many months of searching, he found a master who he believed could help him. On their first day the master invited the professor to his house. They sat down around a table, and the master began to pour tea into the professor's cup. And he poured and he poured and he poured. Soon the tea was ankle deep on the floor. The professor was puzzled but kept quiet, thinking maybe this was the way they did things in the East. Finally, he couldn't keep quiet any longer and said, "Master, my cup has been full for a long time." The master smiled and said, "You're right. You are so full of yourself, what more can I tell you?"

A FEW NIGHTS AGO WHEN I WAS meditating I had a vision. I saw God invite Adam and Eve to tea. After they sat down in his living room and he poured the tea, he said, "I've been working hard these past six days. On the first day I created the eternal light. On the second day, I separated the waters above and below the earth so that the earth was visible. On the third day I created the trees, the flowers, and the grass. On the fourth day, I created the heavenly bodies—the sun, the moon, and the stars. On the fifth day, I created the animals. Yesterday, I created you, Adam and Eve. That's it! I'm tired. I've done enough. From now on it's up to the three of us—you Adam, and you Eve, and me—to finish the job, to finish the creation."

ONCE THERE WAS A GREAT RABBI who for many years had pondered a question, “Where is God?” He asked a friend who was also a rabbi to help him. His friend’s answer was simple, “Wherever and whenever he is invited—that’s where God is.”

WHEN I WAS ELEVEN YEARS OLD and went to Hebrew school (my yeshiva), every Thursday the rabbi would give us a test to find out how much we had learned. On Saturday mornings, before going to the synagogue (my shul) my father would quiz me himself, and in the afternoon my teachers would do it again. One Saturday morning I woke up early and my father according to his custom said, "Let's see what you have learned this week." I was cocky and said to him, "I don't know why you insist on doing this. It's the same text I studied last year. You know I learn my lessons by heart." My father could easily have given me a slap on the head. Instead, he said, "You're right, Chaim, it's the same text you studied last year. But are you the same person you were then?"

In the Garden Of Eden, God was pacing up and down, shaking his head, muttering to himself. The Shekinah, his female counterpart, came over and asked why he was so unhappy. He looked at her, still shaking his head, "Adam and Eve, did you see what they did? They disobeyed me. They did exactly what I told them never to do."The Shekinah was concerned, "God, they're your children. You know what children are. They're just kids—they don't know any better." But God was very angry, "If they don't learn now, they never will. They have to get out of the Garden. They have to go now and be on their own. They have to suffer." The Shekinah tried arguing the children's case for some time, but nothing worked, and finally she gave up, saying, "Okay, have it your way, but if they go, I go too." And she did. She left with Adam and

Eve, and became part of each one of us. God, left alone in the Garden, became very lonely. He had not only lost his children, but his bride. And ever since, he has been mourning, yearning for them to come back home.

A STUDENT ONCE ASKED THE BUDDHA, "Who are you? Are you God?" The Buddha said no. "Are you the son of God?" The Buddha said no. "Are you a saint or a holy man?" The Buddha said no. "What are you?" And the Buddha said, "I'm awake."

THIS IS A STORY ABOUT THE GREAT Rabbi Zusya. When he was dying he gathered his students around his bed and spoke these words: "I know I'm going to see God shortly and I'm not worried. If He asks why I'm not like Moses or a great saint, I'll simply say, 'That's because I'm not Moses and I'm not a saint,' But what if he asks me why I'm not Rabbi Zusya? That's what concerns me most!"

ONCE THERE WAS A LION WHO decided to take a walk along the bank of a great river. Puzzled by the commotion in the water, he looked more closely and realized there was a school of fish in the water desperately swimming to and fro, trying to avoid a fisherman's net. Hoping to help the fish, the lion asked them to come live with him on the land where they'd be safe. The fish shook their heads and said, "No way. If we can't live here in our natural element, how can we live there in yours?"

ONE FRIDAY NIGHT A RABBI CAME home from the synagogue, dragging his steps. He was profoundly weary. When he got home, his wife took one look at him, helped him take off his coat, led him to a chair, and brought him a cup of tea. Only then did she ask him what was wrong. He told her, shaking his head, "It was my sermon about helping the poor for Passover." She was puzzled. What did that have to do with his feeling tired? He shook his head sadly, "The poor are ready to receive right now, but I'm not really sure the rich are ready to give."

ONCE THERE WAS A KING IN PERSIA who was very powerful, but also very unhappy, so unhappy he gathered his advisors around him and asked them for help. They put their heads together and began to argue, but finally came up with a solution. "Your majesty, you must start wearing a shirt that belongs to a happy man. Maybe some of his happiness will pass over to you." So the king commanded his army to go forth and look for a happy man, and they searched and searched and finally found one. The only hitch was he didn't own a shirt at all—he was dressed completely in rags.

CROWTHER

A FEW YEARS AGO A RABBI WENT ON A trip to Rome and was overwhelmed by the magnificence of the old buildings and the statues. He noticed that the statues were covered with tapestries to protect them from the sun, the rain, and the cold. As he stood there in awe, a beggar tugged at his sleeve, asking for a crust of bread. The rabbi looked around once more at the opulence and the grandeur that was Rome and then cried out, "Oh God, here we see statues of stone covered with expensive tapestries, and there we see a living man, created in your own image, covered with rags. A civilization that pays more attention to statues than to human beings will certainly perish."

In Europe many years ago, a woodsman came into the forest with his axe and politely asked the trees to grant him one that he could cut down. This was such a modest request that the oldest trees, an oak and a cedar, immediately acquiesced and gave him an ash tree of no particular importance. However, no sooner had the woodsman cut down the ash tree, he began cutting down all the trees in the forest—even the noblest, oldest ones. The oak tree whispered to the cedar, "Our first concession has cost us everything. If we had not sacrificed our humblest neighbor, we ourselves might have stood for ages."

In Poland there once was a great rabbi, with long white hair and eyes that reflected God's light. One night his followers asked him, "Rebbe, how come all the books you write are so small? All the other rabbis publish books that are huge. Why don't you write a big book?" The wise man replied, "You know my followers are poor people. During the week they work hard sixteen hours a day just to make a living. So come Friday night, they have a meal, go to the synagogue, come home to sleep, and get up early Saturday morning and go to the synagogue again to pray. Then they have another meal, maybe sing a little, and then—only then—they get a little time to read. So if they pick up a big book like the kind the other rebbes write, they'll read maybe one page and then fall asleep. What good is that? But a little book—that's different. A little book they just might finish."

A DISCIPLE ONCE ASKED SWAMI Satchidananda, "How can I gauge how far I am from inner peace?" And the Swami replied, "Make a list of every word you precede with the word, my—my children, my house, my car, my intelligence, my wisdom. If your list is this long (and he spread his arms wide), you are this far from inner peace. If your list is this long (and he held his hands close together), you are this far from inner peace."

ONE NIGHT WHEN I WAS A CHILD I couldn't get to sleep. I kept tossing and turning, and finally asked my soul why. Usually she's very quiet, but that evening she spoke up. "Did you say your prayers?" I was ashamed and told her I hadn't. She shook her head, "Your body is okay—you took a long walk today; your mind is okay—you read a book today; but nothing has been done for me." I realized then that I had neglected her, I had forgotten to say my prayers and had thrown myself out of balance.

Once there was a wealthy Jewish lady who lived on Park Avenue in New York. She was well educated and spoke French and a couple of other languages too. She was about to give birth in Mount Sinai Hospital with three nurses in attendance. Her pain was so great she began to call upon God in French. Her primary nurse was startled—she didn't speak French—and called the woman's doctor, Dr. Schwartz, who simply said, "Let her scream." Two hours later the woman began screaming again, but this time she called on Jesus for help. Again the nurse called Dr. Schwartz who listened and then said, "Let her scream." Several hours later the nurse was back on the phone. "What is she saying now?" Dr. Schwartz asked. The nurse replied, "Shemah Yisrael," (the holiest Jewish prayer). And the doctor answered "I'll be right over."

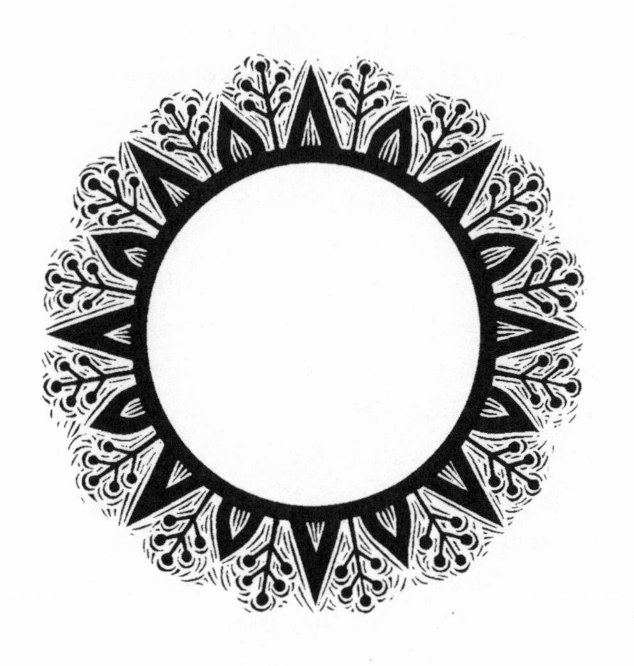

A MAN WHO HID OUT IN A BASEMENT during the Holocaust scratched a Star of David on the wall with the following words: "I believe in the sun, even when it does not shine. I believe in love even when He does not speak."

ONE DAY A YOUNG MAN CAME TO SEE me. HE was—what can I say—a little unbalanced. I could tell by the look in his eyes. He entered my office carrying an armful of books he seemed very attached to. I said, "Please sit down. How can I help you?" "Rabbi," he replied, "I have a very special problem. I'm the Messiah. It says so right here in these books. I've been to the best therapists and the most famous gurus and I've told them so, but nobody believes me." I could see the boy was not altogether there, but my philosophy is that anything is possible. So I said, "Well, it's possible." He thought about it for a minute and then scooped up all his books and left.

Later that night my phone rang. I picked it up and it was his mother. "Rabbi Gelberman, I understand my son came to see you this afternoon." My heart started to sink, "Yes, that's correct." "And I understand that you told him that it's possible he is the Messiah."

Well, I can't lie—after all, I'm a rabbi. So I said, "Well, yes. I did say it's possible," expecting any moment she was going to explode. There was a long silence at the other end of the line, and finally she said, "Tell me, Rabbi, if my son is the Messiah, could it be—is it possible—that I am the mother of the Messiah?"

An extremely devout person, a Hasid, came to complain to his rabbi about two men in the back of the synagogue. "Look at them, Rabbi—they are talking to each other while they are supposed to be praying." And the rabbi replied, "It's the other way around. Even while they are talking to each other, they are praying."

A young Samurai warrior stood respectfully before his Zen master and asked a favor. "I am puzzled. Could you please explain heaven and hell?" The master exploded in rage, "Teach you about heaven and hell? That's ridiculous. You're an ignorant fool—I don't think you could even keep your sword from rusting." At first the young man was surprised, then he got angry, thinking, "Who can insult a Samurai warrior and live?" And with teeth clenched and his blood boiling in fury, he drew his sword. The master looked at him and said gently, "That's hell." The young man thought for a moment, sheathed his sword, and bowed to the master. Looking into his old, beaming face, he felt more love and compassion than he had ever felt in his entire life. And the master raised his finger and said, "That's heaven."

When the founder of Hasidism, the Baal Shem Tov, was alive, whenever the Jews were in danger they would come to him for help. He would then go by himself to a special place in the forest, light a candle, and say a prayer. And the miracle would happen—the Jews would be saved. However, the Baal Shem Tov knew he would die some day, and they probably would not remember the sacred place in the forest, or how to light the flame of the Lord. They might even forget how to pray in times of danger. But there was one thing that the Baal Shem Tov knew his people would never forget, the simple tune he sang when praying with his congregation. It was just a melody without words, but it remained in Jews' hearts long after they forgot the other rituals. So to this day when Jews approach their rabbi for help, he reminds them to sing this simple song or any song which praises God.

ONE BEAUTIFUL SUMMER DAY I WENT to a psychiatric hospital to visit a friend and saw two gentlemen in the front office sitting behind their desks. They were good looking, well dressed men. They looked perfectly normal, like executives at General Motors. Puzzled, wondering what on earth were they doing there, I approached one man and asked why the other man was in a place like this. He looked up from the papers he was reading and said, "Don't you know? He thinks he's Jesus Christ." I said, "How do you know he isn't?" And he answered, "I'm God and I don't even know the guy!"

SOMETIMES WHEN I TEACH THE KABBALAH to my students and talk about the ways we are all connected, even to a homeless person sleeping on the street, I will walk over to one of my pupils and step on his little toe. He'll jump up and ask why I stepped on his toe. I'll look at him and ask him how many toes he has. He'll say ten. Then I'll ask him when was the last time he counted his toes, the last time he thought of that little toe. And then I'll say, "I stepped on your little toe to remind you that it was connected to the other nine toes, and those ten toes were connected to your feet, and your feet to your ankle, and your ankle to your leg, and on and on. That little toe represents everyone we don't really think about, the homeless, the people who are poor, the ones who are sick, the people all over the world who are starving, and in some cases, even our partner, God."

One Friday night at the synagogue the rabbi noticed that a long-standing member of his congregation was talking to himself. The rabbi was alarmed. What if the man was going out of his mind? So he approached the man, "Listen, Yonkel, what's happened to you? I noticed during the service you were arguing with somebody, but nobody was there." The tailor smiled and replied, "To tell you the truth I had a discussion with God." The rabbi asked, "What did you say?" "Well, I said to God, 'Listen, I think you are unfair. You ordered me to fast and repent for my sins. But what sins do I really have? Once in a while I overcharge somebody two cents because I need another piece of bread, but I never lie and I never commit any sins because I don't have the money to do it. You're the sinner, God. You're supposed to be compassionate, but look what you've done to the world. Look at the widows. Look at the orphans. Look at the wars. Look at the hatred that goes on in the world. You are the sinner, I'm not.' But after a minute I relented and told God, 'Listen I'll make a deal with you. If you forgive my sins, I'll forgive yours.'" The rabbi wrung his hands in anguish, "Oh, what a shame! You had God by the neck and you let him off very cheap!"

A HASID WENT TO HIS MASTER COMplaining about his son. "Rabbi, what shall I do with him? He's rebellious, he's violated all the laws—the Bible, the Talmud, and just plain common sense. What shall I do with him?" The master replied, "Love him more."

This is a story my father used to tell me based on the Kabbalah. "While we are sleeping, our souls leave our bodies and go to heaven. There's a night court there and all the souls must attend to report on their activities that day. Some of the souls get permission to return to their bodies. Others do not—they are the ones who die during the night."

THERE WAS A YOUNG BOY ABOUT eleven or twelve years old who fell in love with a pretty young girl. He approached her father to ask his permission to marry her. The father was surprised, but decided to play along. "You want to marry my daughter? How are you going to live?" The boy thought carefully for a moment and replied, "I have a nice room, but your daughter has a bigger one, so we are going to live here with you." The man hid a smile with his hand, "And how do you plan on supporting her?" The boy had his answer ready. It was obvious he had thought through every problem. "I get about ten dollars a month for my allowance and she gets twenty—thirty dollars should be enough for us to live on." The man was so surprised and pleased by the boy's cleverness he pushed the issue further. “What if you have children? How are you going to support them?” The boy replied without blinking, “So far we haven’t been lucky, but we’re trying.”

AN AMERICAN JEW WENT TO EUROPE to visit an Hasidic rabbi, an old friend. They hadn't seen each other for thirty years. They sat down and had lunch together. During the ensuing conversation, the American kept inquiring about people he knew in the town, "How's Rabbi Yonkel?" "Dead," said the rabbi as he continued to concentrate on his food. The American nodded sadly, "And how's Rabbi Shlomo?" "Dead," said the Rabbi chewing slowly on his slice of bread. The conversation, such as it was, continued for a while until the frustrated American became impatient and exploded, "Is everyone here dead?" The rabbi looked up and said calmly, "Only when I'm eating."

EVERYONE WHO KNEW DORA, MY WIFE, knew she was a very good cook. She also was a smart lady—she ran a settlement house in downtown New York. Every Passover we'd invite a lot of people for a Seder. Most of them looked forward to eating her matzo ball soup, which was very tasty. She knew this and spent a lot of time preparing it. However, on this particular Passover, Dora was so busy at the office she didn't have time to prepare it, so she bought some packaged soup and did something with it (I don't know what exactly) and it tasted very good. That night at the Seder, one of the guests asked her, "Did you make this soup? It's delicious." Now Dora had a problem. She was a rabbi's wife and it was Passover. She didn't want to tell the truth, and she didn't want to lie. So she said, "You know, on Passover, you're only allowed to ask four questions."

DO YOU KNOW WHO MOSES WAS? HE was the man who spoke directly to God, who talked to the Pharaoh, who led his people out of bondage and steered them safely through forty years of exile. There are many adjectives the Old Testament uses to describe this man. And how does the Bible speak of Moses? Simply this way: "Moses was a humble man."

IN THE OLD DAYS IN EUROPE, ORTHODOX rabbis didn't get a salary. Instead, they served as lawyers and judges in their towns. When Jews had problems, no matter how difficult, they wouldn't go to a civil court—they would go to a rabbinical court, and whoever lost the case would pay the rabbi. That is how rabbis made their living. One particular rabbi was known for his compassion—he would tell people not to make an issue out of their problem. "Let's go into my study instead of the courtroom, and we'll arbitrate the matter. We don't want one Jew fighting another Jew." So he would arbitrate and never lost a case. Therefore nobody had to pay him. One day the rabbi's wife who was tired of being poor said to her husband, "If everybody is going to be right, how are we going to eat?" He looked at her and replied, "You know, my dear, you're right too."

AFTER ADAM AND EVE COMMITTED their sin, God's first words were, "Where are you?" This puzzled me at first. Didn't He know where they were? After all there were just those two people in the Garden of Eden. God certainly knew they were hiding, but he didn't want to know what part of the garden they were in. He meant, "What kind of person are you to disobey me?" Whenever you begin meditating, try to hear God talking to you. If you listen carefully, you will hear Him saying, "Where are you? Where is your love when you see another person walking down the street? Don't you know that my spirit is within that person. You must constantly ask yourself, 'Where am I?'"

THERE ONCE WAS A JEWISH WOMAN who lived with her mother in Queens in New York City. She was thirty-five years old and wanted to get married. Finally she fell in love. The only problem was the man was Christian. Her mother got very angry and refused to talk to her about it, and whenever they did talk about it, they usually began to fight. Finally the daughter came to me for counseling. After I heard her story, I asked her to describe an argument she had had with her mother in detail, and I began to understand. Her mother was brought up in an orthodox Jewish family and was taught that it's simply not kosher to have a Christian son-in-law, while the daughter was trying to convince her mother that an interfaith marriage was perfectly all right. As a way of solving this impasse, I said, "I'll tell you what to do. The next time you have a fight with your mother, smile at her and say, 'You know, Mother, you're right. If I were in your shoes I would feel the same way.'" The approach worked like a miracle. After that one conversation there were no more fights and her mother even came to the wedding! Those simple words made her mother feel she hadn't lived a lie all her life.

777
19
2/1071
$100—
Dollars
778
Dollars

A SALESMAN WAS ON HIS WAY TO A BIG city. It was pretty late in the day and he was tired so he decided to stop and spend the night in a small village. The next morning he went to the synagogue, expecting to say a few quick prayers and leave. However, the service took longer than he expected. When it was over, he gave a hundred dollar bill to the rabbi, saying, "Your sermon was unbelievable." The rabbi thanked him, but added, "I'm puzzled—I saw you sleep through my whole sermon. How could you say it was unbelievable?" The salesman was happy to explain. "That's the point, Rabbi. I suffer from insomnia and have gone to the best doctors, but nobody has been able to help me. But you, the minute you began to talk, I slept better than I have in weeks."

Once there was a wealthy rabbi with a beautiful young daughter he wanted to marry off, so he asked the head of the yeshiva to send over three of his best students.

So one at a time, the young men came over to the rabbi's house on Friday night to have dinner with the rabbi and his family. The following afternoon, the rabbi would take the student out for a walk and on that walk he would ask him the following question: "Tell me son, if there was a thousand dollar bill lying on the ground and it's Saturday (when Jews are not allowed to touch money), would you pick it up?"

The first student said, "It's the Sabbath, and I wouldn't do it." And the rabbi sent him back to the yeshiva with a polite note, "Although I like the boy, I don't think he's smart enough."

The second student came the following Friday night and the next day took a walk with the rabbi who asked him the same question. The student replied, "That thousand dollar bill is just a piece of paper. So what if it says a thousand dollars? It's no sin to pick up a piece of paper on the Sabbath. I'd pick it up." The rabbi sent him back too with a nice letter. "This is a very smart boy, but I don't think he's religious enough."

The third student went through the same routine, and after taking some time, found his answer, "Let me see the thousand dollar bill with my own eyes and I'll make up my mind."

This was the boy who won the rabbi's daughter.

When I was a young boy in Hungary, my father taught me an important lesson. He owned a big department store, and one day while we were at the synagogue, his store was broken into, looted, and set on fire. And to make it worse, he found out it was our neighbors who did it! But it was the Sabbath and on the Sabbath you don't talk about business. So we continued with our prayers. That night we finally talked about it. He wasn't the least bit angry. "We have to build the store again. This is our home. What else can we do? If I lose my store and allow my blood pressure to rise, that is paying double. I don't believe in paying twice."

NOT BEING AWARE OF THE ANGELS' presence in our lives is like having an uncle in California who's a billionaire who died and left you millions of dollars. Unless you're aware of that uncle, you're never going to get that money.

ONCE THERE WAS A RABBI WHO CAME out of the synagogue on Yom Kippur, the day of atonement when Jews fast. And to his surprise, on this solemn day, he saw one of his students eating. He went up to him and said, “Joseph, don’t you know what day it is? You’re not supposed to eat.” And Joseph answered politely, “I know, but I’m hungry.” The rabbi looked at the sandwich and was shocked, “It’s ham. You’re eating ham, a forbidden food, on a day when you’re not supposed to eat at all!” And Joseph said, “I know. I was hungry.” The rabbi looked up to heaven, raised his hands to God and said imploringly, “Please, God, give Joseph credit for not lying.”

RECENTLY I WAS INVITED TO AN interfaith marriage held in a Roman Catholic church in Manhattan. The bride's family was Catholic, but she had fallen in love with a Jewish man. It was his grandmother who invited me to the wedding. The priest who was officiating at the wedding approached me and said, "Rabbi, the father of the bride would like you to use as little Hebrew as possible when you give your speech." He wanted me to speak in English! That bothered me. I replied, "Tell the father of the bride that I will not do so. I'll speak in Hebrew because I want Jesus to understand what we are doing here."

C.R. CROWTHER

WHY DID GOD WAIT UNTIL THE sixth day to create Adam and Eve? Why didn't he create them on the first day, Sunday? Here's my explanation. If he created them on that day, you may be sure that by Monday or Tuesday they'd have created a committee to tell God how to proceed.

ONE NIGHT I HAD A DREAM IN WHICH I died and woke up in heaven. To my surprise, I was greeted by angels who knew my name. I was startled and told them, "Listen, I'm not going to stay. I just came to visit." The archangel Michael approached me and asked, "Whom would you like to see?" After I thought for a moment (the question was important), I said, "I'd like to see the Messiah who was born out of the house of King David. I want to talk to him." The angels took me into a beautiful room where I saw, to my great surprise, dozens of messiahs. In the middle of the group was the Messiah Jews are waiting for. To his right Jesus was seated, to his left Mohammed, and surrounding them were Krishna, Buddha, and other redeemers from different religions. They all greeted me and Jesus said, "What would you like to ask me?" I had one simple question, "Do you know what's happening on earth, the disease, wars, conflict? At least one of you should come—I don't care which one." Krishna spoke up, "Rabbi, you've forgotten the Kabbalah. For years you've been teaching people they are partners with God. We're ready to come, all you have to do is invite us."

A FAMOUS RABBI GOT TIRED OF HEARING the members of his congregation tell him their worries. Finally he laughed and said, “Instead of saying, ‘What if so and so happens?’, try saying, ‘So what if so and so happens!’”

IN THE OLD DAYS RABBIS WOULD SIT WITH their students on Saturday night before the service and talk. According to Jewish law they were not allowed to switch on the electricity until the Sabbath ended. So they would sit in the dark with their students, and to pass the time they would spin tall tales about their masters. And of course the students would never dare to question anything the rabbis said. On this particular night a rabbi told a story that was totally unbelievable. A student who wasn't too bright was shocked and couldn't keep his mouth shut. When the Sabbath was over, he approached the rabbi and asked whether the story was true. The rabbi found himself in a dilemma. He didn't want to lie, particularly on the Sabbath, and he couldn't tell the truth either. His answer was one I often use: "It could have been true."

THE OTHER DAY I SAID JOKINGLY TO a couple of friends, "When I die, I'd rather go to hell." They were flabbergasted. "What are you saying, Rabbi?" I explained, "What would I have to do in heaven? Who would need me? There are so many learned men and scholars there. No, maybe in hell I could go on teaching."

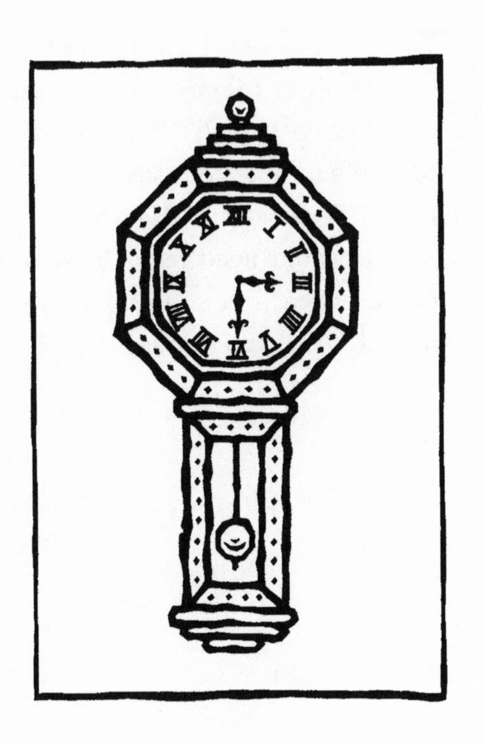

ONCE THERE WAS A MAN WHO CAME to the rabbi's house one Saturday afternoon and listened to him discoursing on the Torah. He was a very rude person and kept interrupting the rabbi until finally the rabbi for the first time in his life lost his temper and ordered the man out of his house. That night God came into the rabbi's dream in the form of a angel and told him, "Rabbi, I'm disappointed in you. I've put up with this man for over fifty years, and you can't put up with him for half an hour?"

THERE IS AN INTERESTING STATEMENT by God in the Book of Creation, "It is not good for man to be alone. I shall make him a partner." Who do you think said that? Adam? For all we know he was probably a happy bachelor. After all, he didn't complain about being single. It was God who was unhappy, not Adam. God knew the pain of loneliness—He too was alone before He created Adam.

DAG HAMMARSKJOLD, FORMER HEAD of the United Nations, said, "The longest journey of the soul is inward." The journey begins with attitude. We can defile the most exquisite temple with a rigid attitude, and we can sanctify a mud puddle if we see the reflection of a star in it.

100

A PRIEST, A RABBI, AND A PROTESTANT minister were the best of friends. One day the three of them were having coffee and the question came up how they handled the money collected during services. The priest spoke up first saying that he had a big circle drawn on top of his desk and when the collection plate was taken to his office, he threw the money into the circle. "Whatever remains inside the circle belongs to God, whatever falls outside the circle I use for my own expenses." The minister said he had a similar system, except instead of a circle he had a line drawn on his desk, not a circle. "Whatever falls on the right side of the line belongs to God—the rest is mine." The rabbi listened carefully to his two friends and then offered his own system. "When I get the plate I throw it up into the air. Whatever stays in the air belongs to God."

ONCE THERE WAS A VERY RICH Jewish man who died and left a lot of money not only to his synagogue, but also to a Catholic church and a Protestant one. He was covering his bets. He left a message in his will that he would appreciate it if the three clergymen would eulogize him. Needless to say, all three clergymen attended his funeral and spoke during the services. The first man to speak was the priest who talked for about an hour because the dead man had given a lot of money to the Catholic Church. Next the Protestant minister spoke for an hour and a half because the deceased had given even more money to his church. Last, the rabbi climbed up to the podium and spoke for about three hours, because the dead man was the biggest supporter of his synagogue. When he was almost through, the rabbi looked at his watch and said, "I have to stop soon—it's time for me to attend services in our synagogue."

Suddenly the coffin sprang open, and the dead man grabbed hold of the rabbi's coat, pleading with him, "Rabbi, you forgot to mention how humble I was."

THERE WERE TWO RABBINICAL SCHOOLS of thought in ancient Israel about one issue. One school argued that taking into consideration all the problems and frustrations of life, it might be better not to be born at all. The other school argued that despite the anxiety, sickness, and tragedies, it's still good to be alive. They engaged in a debate on this issue for two and a half years, and finally came to a unanimous conclusion. Do you know what it was? They agreed that is it better not to have been born, but since birth is inevitable, a wise person must find meaning and purpose in his or her life, despite all the hardships and setbacks. Otherwise life is a waste and so is this argument.

A GREAT PHILOSOPHER CAME TO Jerusalem and stopped a little child on the street. "Son, I'll give you a gold coin if you tell me where God is." The child looked up at the tall stranger and replied, "Mister, I'll give you two gold coins if you tell me where God is not."

THERE IS A STORY ABOUT RABBI Akiba, one of the greatest of all rabbis. He was the son of a very poor man and was making his living as a water carrier in Jerusalem. One day he was delivering water to a very rich man in that city and saw a woman observing him from a window. It was love at first sight in both directions—Akiba was very handsome and the woman was very beautiful. Akiba, who was not at all shy, went up to the woman and asked her to marry him. She laughed, replying, "Do you know who my father is? Me marry a water carrier? He'd fall over, laughing." But Akiba refused to be humiliated. He smiled and said, "Don't worry about it. It's not a big problem." And the next day he quit his job and enrolled in a Hebrew school. Imagine a room filled with five year olds with Akiba fitting himself into a very small desk. However, he never felt bad about it. He simply studied hard, learned the Hebrew alphabet, and studied the ancient Hebrew texts. He rapidly became a great scholar and within a few years became the greatest rabbi in the city of Jerusalem and later throughout Israel. And, in case I forget, yes, he did marry the woman who had scorned him.

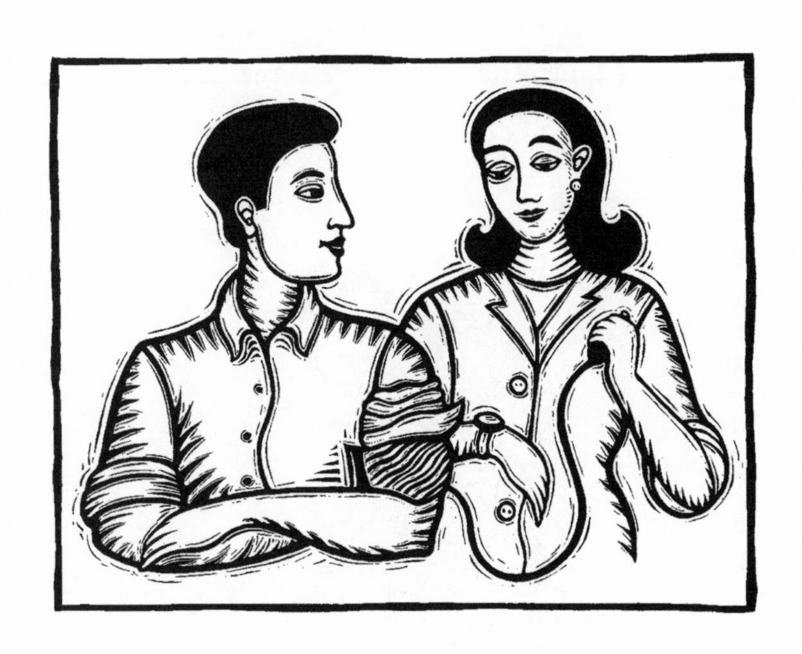

When I officiate at Jewish weddings I always explain to the newlyweds the significance of the groom's stamping on a glass. It's a way of reminding the couple that when they argue, instead of breaking each other's heart they can simply break a glass. One day I met a couple that I had married ten years before and asked how things were going. "Beautiful," the man replied. "We have three children and everything is wonderful. But"(he added with a grin) "we have no dishes left."

A RABBI AND A PRIEST WERE THE BEST of friends and had tea together frequently. They loved each other's company and took turns—one time in the priest's house and the next in the rabbi's. One day as they were drinking their tea, the priest looked at the rabbi and said, "I swear to you, Joseph, you are a Christian." And the rabbi replied, "What makes me in your eyes a Christian, makes you in my eyes a Jew."

IT IS WRITTEN IN THE OLD TESTAMENT that "This is a day of light and a day of joy, a day of peace and total harmony." Rabbis in the old days puzzled over this passage, wondering what day it referred to. The answer came back from God. This day—today—is the only day we have. Yesterday is gone and tomorrow is uncertain.

Jews celebrate the Sabbath on Saturday. Later on the Christians, who were mostly Jews but followed Christ's teachings, felt uncomfortable celebrating their holy day the same way, so they decided to look for another day and chose Sunday. Seven hundred years later, the Muslims had five days to choose from and took Friday as their Sabbath. I suggest that Christians and Jews join the Muslims in their mosques on Friday, Muslims and Christians join the Jews in their synagogues on Saturday, and the Jews and Muslims join the Christians in their churches on Sunday. Wouldn't it be wonderful? It could usher in the Messianic age.

A STRANGER ARRIVED IN A SMALL TOWN and saw a group of people coming out of a house singing and dancing. He tapped one of the people on the shoulder and asked him what was happening and was told that they were celebrating the birth of a child. The next day he saw people coming out of a house crying. Again he asked what was happening and learned that someone had just died. He pondered this for a while, scratching his beard, and said, "It should be the other way around. When a baby is born, you don't know what's going to happen to that child. He might become a wicked man, like Hitler. The real celebration should happen when people die—a celebration of all the wonderful things they did with their lives. It is not the setting out on a voyage that should be celebrated, but the successful return."

WHEN MY FAMILY WAS TAKEN FROM me during the Holocaust, I asked the question a million times, "Why?" and there never was any answer. When I started to ask myself "How?" (How do I deal with this, how can I go on living now?), little by little I was able to find an answer, to concentrate on the solution rather than the problem. And I dedicated my life to teaching people of all faiths how to believe in God, to love God, and to walk with God, and to love their neighbors as they love themselves.

ONCE THERE WERE TWO BROTHERS who lived in the Holy Land. They worked together and tilled the soil together. One was married with a big family, the other was single. Each year they divided the harvest equally. Afterward, the single brother thought, "I have taken my half of the harvest, but I don't need it. I have no wife, no children—my brother needs it more." So that night he couldn't sleep, he got up and loaded his wagon, and he drove to the other side of the mountain where his brother lived and left a portion of his half of the harvest there. The married brother couldn't sleep either, worrying about his brother growing old with no one to take care of him. So he too got up in the middle of the night and left a portion of his half of the harvest in his brother's barn. In the morning, they were puzzled, they could not understand what had happened. The next night they met right in the middle of the mountain that separated their land. As they saw each other, they understood what had happened, got off their wagons, embraced, and kissed each other. According to Hasidic tradition, God observed their meeting and said, "This is the place where I want my temple built."

Life is not living in a waiting room—
it's waiting in a living room.